Canning For Kids

The Canning and Preserving Adventure

by
Well-Being Publishing

To You,

Thank you!

Table of Contents

Introduction:
Welcome to Canning!

Welcome, curious minds and budding chefs! Have you ever wondered how pickles keep their crunch or how jam stays sweet and spreadable all year round? Well, you're in for a treat because you're about to embark on a delicious adventure into the world of canning!

Yes, canning! It's like packing all the flavors of summer in a jar so you can enjoy it even when the leaves start to crunch under your boots. Some people might think it's an old-timey thing that only grandmas do, but guess what? They're missing out! Canning is cool, creative, and, believe it or not, a total game-changer for your taste buds!

So, what's canning all about? It's taking all that awesome goodness from fruits, veggies, and even meats, and locking it down tight in a jar to keep it safe and tasty. It's a magical kitchen adventure where you'll become a food wizard, armed with pots, ladles, and jars, ready to capture and preserve the essence of food.

But hey, I get it. You might be thinking, "That sounds like tricky business." Don't worry! We're going to go step by step like dancing through the most fun food-filled dance floor ever. You'll learn how to squish strawberries into jam, turn cucumbers into the crunchiest pickles, and transform tomatoes into the sauciest salsa you've ever tasted.

And it's way more than making snacks; it's about munching on knowledge nuggets too. You'll be a pro at understanding the why behind the yum. Ever pondered why certain foods spoil? Or how heat messes with microbes? You'll be filling your brain as much as filling your jars!

For all you junior scientists out there, canning is also a blast of a science experiment. You'll witness the power of heat, the might of sugar, vinegar, and salt, and the airtight seal – all working together to keep your food fresh as the day it was picked!

But slow your rolls for a second; we have to talk safety. You might not be juggling chainsaws, but safety is key in the kitchen, especially when canning. Don't fret – I'll guide you through all the must-dos and no-nos to keep you and your creations safe and sound.

Perhaps you're wondering, "Where do I even begin?" Well, we've got you covered! We'll talk about the tools of the trade. From the simplest spoon to the most sophisticated canning funnel, you'll know what you need and how to use it.

And if you're feeling artsy-fartsy, canning is like crafting – but you get to eat your art! Imagine layering colors and flavors in a jar, making each one a masterpiece that also tastes amazing. Plus, we've got some genius gifting ideas that'll make your canned concoctions the talk of the town.

Canning isn't just a solo mission; it's a community fiesta! You can share the love by trading recipes, throwing canning parties, or joining a canning club. Just picture it: you and your friends making memories and munchies together – how sweet is that?!

Now, for all you planet protectors and green-hearted warriors, caning is also about sustainable living. We're talking less waste, more taste, and a high-five to Mother Nature. You'll learn how growing your ingredients can be part of this eco-awesome cycle.

As we journey from garden to jar, you'll see that canning isn't just a chore – it's a celebration! A celebration of flavors, of seasons, and of a job well-done. And before you know it, you'll be taking a peek into that pantry of yours, grinning from ear to ear at the rows of colorful jars, each holding a story, a memory, and a burst of homemade deliciousness.

Are you ready to roll up your sleeves, wield your wooden spoon like a magic wand, and dive headfirst into the sticky, sweet, and sensational world of canning? Let's stir up some fun and infuse every jar with a little bit of love and lots of flavors. Welcome to canning, where the jar is just the beginning!

Chapter 1:
What is Canning?

Imagine you could capture a pocket of sunshine, the essence of summer, and a taste explosion—all in a single jar. Well, guess what? That's canning in a nutshell! It's like a magic show in your kitchen where fruits and veggies are the stars, and jars are their stage. Canning is the superhero method of preserving food, saving the day (and the harvest) by locking in flavors, nutrients, and all the good stuff in food that makes your taste buds dance. It's a time-traveling adventure that lets you whoosh fresh produce into the future. And it's not just old-timey pioneer stuff; it's a cool craft for you to flex your chef muscles, munch on healthier snacks, and zing your meals with homemade amazingness. Plus, bonus points—it's like giving a high-five to Mother Earth by reducing waste. So, let's pop the lid off this jar of wonders and dive into the scrumptious world of canning!

Understanding Preserving Food

So, what's the big deal about keeping your eats from going bad? Think of it like this: long ago, before fridges were a thing, folks had to get crafty to make their food last longer. Canning is like a superhero for strawberries and peas, zapping them into a state of delicious 'pause'! You're packing fruits, veggies, and other yum-yums into jars, and then using heat to kick out the spoilage-causing micro-mini-monsters (a.k.a. bacteria). It's like throwing an exclusive party in a jar, and only the tasty nutrients and flavors are on the guest list. The heat seals the deal, making sure nothing nasty crashes the bash. And voilà, you've got green beans and peach jam that can hang out in your pantry for ages, just waiting to join your next meal or midnight snack. It's a cool way to embrace the magic of the olden days, give a high-five to Mother Earth by wasting less food, and hey, it's a sneaky science lesson too!

The History of Canning is as fascinating as it is flavorful, jam-packed with ingenious ideas and bursting with juicy facts that'll stick with you like peach preserves on fresh toast! So, here's how this all began—gather 'round for a story that's as old as time... well, not quite that old, but certainly ripe with history!

The tale takes us back to the late 18th century, when the French government was in a pickle of its own. They needed a way to feed their hungry soldiers and sailors during long military campaigns. None other than Napoleon Bonaparte offered a cash reward for anyone who could come up with a reliable food preservation method. And guess who showed up to the food fight? A candy maker and brewer named Nicolas Appert!

This food visionary took the challenge head-on. He didn't have fancy gadgets or high-tech equipment, but what he did have were glass jars, a cauldron, and ambition. Nicolas discovered that if he put food into jars, sealed them with wax, and then heated them, the food didn't spoil. Voilà! His technique paved the path for what we now know as canning. But, hold your horses: it wasn't called canning just yet, as he used bottles, not cans.

Now, while Nicolas was sealing up jars in France, over in England, Peter Durand was taking notes. He snagged himself a patent in 1810 for using tin cans instead of glass jars. These cans weren't like the ones we know today. Imagine a whopping great thing that needed a hammer and chisel to open it—yep, no handy pull-tabs back then!

Let's speed up the time machine a bit to the 1850s, where an American inventor by the name of Gail Borden introduced condensed milk in—you guessed it—cans. His ingenuity during a time without refrigerators meant milk could travel far and wide without going sour. Families could enjoy milk with their cookies for much longer!

However, it's not just the inventors who deserve a round of applause. The can opener finally made its entrance in 1858, meaning people could access their canned goods without the risk of flying metal scraps. And let's not forget the housewives, cooks, and local grocers who hopped on the canning wagon, sealing up seasonal fruits and veggies to brighten up winter meals.

As we fast-forward to the 20th century, canning took another leap forward. It boogied its way into pop art history thanks to Andy Warhol's famous Campbell's soup cans. And speaking of soup, during the World Wars, canned goods became the hero on the home front, serving up sustenance to families and soldiers alike.

The victory gardens during World War II also played a significant role in canning history. Folks grew their veggies and canned the bounties to support the war effort. They were like superheroes, with pots and pans for shields and ladles for lances, battling the food scarcity villain!

Flash to the peace and love era of the 70s—canning had a revival with the back-to-the-land movement. Folks wanted to reconnect with their food sources and canning provided the perfect way to preserve the natural goodness of home-grown produce.

Now, bubbling over to modern-day magic, canning isn't just for survival—it's for thrival! (Okay, so that's not a word, but if it were, canning would be in its definition!) It's become a culinary art, a crafty hobby for foodies, and a way for you to wield the power of preservation right in your kitchen.

So, here's the thing, canning has come a long way from its humble beginnings. It's equipped with better safety standards and more precise methods. Smarter and more creative techniques have opened up a whole pantry of possibilities!

Why does all this matter, you might wonder? Well, knowing the ins and outs of canning's past can inspire us to appreciate the food on our shelves and to innovate in our munchy masterpieces. Plus, isn't it just cool to think you're part of a story that spans centuries?

The history of canning demonstrates how ingenuity and necessity have shaped the way we eat. Each canned good is a time capsule, capturing a moment in history, keeping it fresh and tasty for days, months, even years to come.

So, whenever you pop open a new jar of strawberry jam or twist open a can of soup, think of it as opening a page in the grand book of canning history. You're not just enjoying delicious preserves; you're savoring a legacy that's been handed down through ages—one that you, too, can pass on.

With every squish of tomatoes into sauce or each batch of berries turned into jam, remember: you're carrying the torch that folks like Nicolas Appert and Peter Durand lit over 200 years ago. And who knows? Maybe one of your canning creations will make history someday. Ready, set, preserve!

Why We Can: Benefits for Today Okay, let's peel the lid off this idea of canning and dig into why it's still super cool—and important—for us today! Sure, your grandparents probably canned out of necessity, but there are a bunch of fresh reasons why canning is making a comeback, sprouting up in kitchens quicker than you can say "pickle my peppers!"

First off, let's talk taste. When you preserve your own food, you're the boss of flavor town. Forget those bland, store-bought cans packed with who-knows-what kind of preservatives. Canning lets you capture the peak freshness and yumminess of fruits and veggies, plus you can jazz them up with your favorite herbs and spices. It's like crafting a flavor playlist that'll have your taste buds dancing every time you pop open a jar.

And you know what? Canning is kind of like a superhero when it comes to fighting waste. Think of all those delicious berries you picked last summer that went bad before you could turn them into smoothies. When you can, you're saving food from being trashed and turning it into treasure. Less waste, more taste—that's a motto we can all get behind!

Here's a thought: canning can save you some serious cash. Yeah, those pennies add up! Instead of buying pricey preservatives or out-of-season produce that's traveled more miles than a rock band on tour, canning lets you stock up on what's local and affordable. Then, when winter rolls around, you've got a pantry full of goodies that didn't break the bank. Cha-ching!

Canning is also a secret handshake into the cool club of creativity. Mix and match fruits for a jam that's as unique as you are or invent a pickle potion that'll impress even the pickiest of pals. It's like being a kitchen wizard, with jars instead of wands and fruits instead of spells. Abracadabra, deliciousness!

But wait, let's be real. Canning has some serious street cred when it comes to health. By doing it yourself, you're kicking added sugars and salts to the curb. You have the power to keep your goodies as natural as a squirrel gathering nuts—except you're gathering peaches, peppers, or pears. Healthy choices in a jar? That's what's up!

Ever heard of DIY? Of course, you have! Well, canning is DIY to the max. It's you showing the world that, yes, you can whip up incredible eats without needing a trip to the store. It's about rolling up your sleeves and feeling that awesome pride when you say, "Yup, I made that!" The DIY spirit has never tasted so good.

Let's not forget about our dear planet Earth. Every jar you fill is a win for Mother Nature. Buying local produce to can supports your community's farmers, and reduces all the transport hullabaloo that comes with food that's been on a worldwide tour. We're talking fewer food miles, less pollution, and a happier planet. Win-win, am I right?

Moreover, canning is the time machine of the food world. Open a jar of strawberry jam in the middle of winter, and bam! You're instantly transported back to the sunny fields of June. It's like bottling sunbeams, only it's berries, and you can actually taste them. Time travel has never been so easy—or tasty!

What about those zombie apocalypse movies where everyone's hunting for food? Well, when you can, you're basically prepping for anything—storms, power outages, or just those nights when you can't face the grocery store. Your pantry turns into a treasure trove of ready-to-eat delights, no matter what life throws at you.

Plus, canning is a chance to weave some real magic by creating traditions. Imagine making your grandma's famous apple butter and passing it down through generations. Each jar isn't just filled with food, but also with stories, memories, and love. It's tradition packed in syrup and sealed with a family secret.

You also become a bit of a time manager with canning. By preserving batches of food when they're in abundance, you're spreading out the prep work throughout the year. This means more free time and less stress during busy meal times. It's like you're gifting Future You with the luxury of extra minutes—or hours. Future You is already thanking you!

Safety is a big deal when you're in the kitchen, and canning introduces you to super important skills like sterilization and food safety. These aren't just good for canning; they're life skills, folks! You'll be leveling up in kitchen responsibility like a pro. Who knew canning could turn you into a food safety champion?

Speaking of skills, let's talk about those handy-dandy life lessons. Canning isn't just about preserving food; it's about patience, precision, and perseverance. There's no app for peeling apples or simmering sauces—it's just you, the food, and the journey to Jarville. It's a process that teaches you that some of the best things in life take time and effort.

Finally, canning is an adventure. Each fruit or veggie you decide to jar is like setting off on a new culinary quest. Whether it's exploring exotic spice islands for your peach chutney or braving the great outdoors for wild blackberries, canning is your ticket to flavor exploration. And who doesn't love a good adventure, especially when you can eat it afterward?

So, there you have it, friends—canning is not just a relic of the past; it's a path to tasty, healthy, creative, sustainable, and downright fun living. It's perfect for you, your family, and this great big world we call home. Now let's get those jars ready and begin a fabulous food adventure together!

Chapter 2:
Canning Safety First

Now that we've dipped our toes in the fascinating pool of canning, let's paddle over to the shallow end and talk safety, because nobody wants a kitchen mishap, especially when you're handling jars that are hotter than a sunny day in July! Remember, in the world of canning, cleanliness is not just next to godliness; it's essential for keeping those wicked foodborne villains at bay. We're going to be like food safety superheroes, donning our capes of caution and using our powers of sterilization to fight off unwanted bacteria. So, we'll be making sure everything is spick-and-span before we get to show those fruits and veggies who's boss. You'll learn to handle hot pots and jars like a pro, and we'll go over the no-nos that keep you safe, sound, and ready to enjoy your delicious creations. It's not just about making your pantry look like a rainbow of yummy jars – it's about doing it safely so that every scrumptious bite is as safe as it is sensational!

The Rules of Safe Canning

Now that we've dipped our toes into the bubbling pot of canning, let's turn up the heat with some scorching-hot rules for keeping things safe! Before you start mashing berries or slicing cucumbers, pump the brakes! Safety's the name of the game, and it's way cooler than a game of hot potato with a glass jar. Always remember that clean jars are happy jars, so scrub-a-dub-dub those glass soldiers and keep them germ-free with sterilization (which we'll jump into like a pool on a hot day later in the chapter). Keep your fingers from a burn dance by using proper tools—tongs are not just a weird word, they're your best buds in the canning world. Your ingredients should be fresher than your favorite joke, so pick the cream of the crop. Low-acid and high-acid foods party differently in the canning club; they each have their VIP rules to follow, or you'll be crashing the party. Seal the deal right by checking for the pop! It's like getting a high-five from your jar, saying, 'You did it!' And last, let's keep the 'pressure' in pressure canning and not on you; so take your time, learn as you go, and remember, a watched pot never boils, but an unwatched pot makes a mess—don't go wandering off! Stick to the plan, and we'll keep those jars jiving safely on your pantry shelf!

Sterilization: Why So Clean? Okay, superstars of the canning universe, have you ever wondered why your kitchen turns into a science lab when you start canning? Well, it's all about keeping your food safe and tasty for as long as possible. Sterilization isn't just a fancy word; it's kind of like the superhero of canning, swooping in to save the day from tiny villains called microbes. Microbes are like invisible bugs that love to crash your food's shelf-life party. And unlike actual party crashers, you can't ask them to leave; you've got to be a bit more...creative.

Imagine a teeny-tiny world, much smaller than a crumb. In this world, microbes play hide and seek all day. Sounds kinda cute, right? Except these little guys are not the kind of guests you want hiding in your peach jam. If they get in and get comfy, they can spoil your food – and not in a "Whoops, I used salt instead of sugar" kind of way. We're talking about a "pickles tasting like gym socks" situation. Gross, right?

The reason we clean and sterilize everything is like a one-two punch against these invisible mischief-makers. Zap! Pow! By cleaning, we take away their favorite playgrounds, and by sterilizing, we turn those playgrounds into no-bug zones. It's doing a big favor for your future self who will be enjoying all the deliciousness you've canned without unwelcome surprises.

But wait, there's more! Have you ever seen a little bubble trapped in the jam you've just bought? That's a sign that the jar has been sterilized. By taking the time to carefully clean and heat your jars, you push out the air and create a vacuum seal when it cools down. This seal acts like a super-strong barrier against any new bugs that want to join the party. It's like having the best bouncer at the club door of your jar.

Now, you might think, "I clean my room, so I know how to clean," right? Well, sterilizing is next-level cleaning. It's like if your room was clean enough for a family of teeny astronauts to live in. That's how clean we want our jars to be.

Here's a pro tip: Sterilizing isn't hard. You'll boil some water, take a dip (I mean, your jars will take a dip), and you're halfway there. It's a bit like giving your jars a hot bath before they go to bed, tucked in with all that yummy food for a long nap on your shelf.

And don't think it's just the jars that need a good cleaning. Everything that touches your food needs the sterilization superpower. Utensils, lids, countertops - think of them as guests at your canning party. You want them all sparkling clean so they can serve up some good times without any bouts of food troubles later.

One more thing – be patient and thorough. Rushing sterilization is like skipping the climax in a movie. You wouldn't do that, right? The buildup is important, so give the process the time it needs. Rushing leads to shortcuts, and shortcuts lead to...you guessed it, possible gym socks pickles. And nobody, absolutely nobody, wants that.

Let's take a closer look at those lids, shall we? Lids are super important because they make the seal that keeps the air out and the goodness in. They've got this special sealing compound around the edge that needs to be heated to work its magic. When it cools, it holds on to the jar like a koala on a tree branch, all snug and secure.

Now, you might wonder what happens if you skip sterilizing your jars and lids. Imagine inviting a friend over to your house without cleaning. They walk in and boom – it's untidy, it's a bit smelly, totally embarrassing, right? That's what happens to your food if you skip sterilization. Bacteria and mold jump in, and they don't mind the mess. In fact, they love it. So do yourself a favor and clean up before the party.

Sterilizing also gives you peace of mind. When you twist open that jar of strawberry jam in the middle of winter, you don't want to be crossing your fingers, hoping it's still good. You want to be absolutely sure. And you can be sure if you've followed the superhero sterilization steps. Confidence – that's what clean jars give you!

Now, for all the young chefs in the house, here's an analogy you'll appreciate. Think of your canning jar as your personal video game character. Before you enter the Boss Level (which, in our world, is the Canning Level), you'd gear up, right? Sterilizing is like equipping your character with the best armor. Without it, your character won't stand a chance against the boss's attacks – or in our world, against the microscopic baddies.

Also, remember to let everything cool down properly. Just like you shouldn't touch a cookie tray right out of the oven, don't rush into handling sterilized jars and tools. They're hot, hot, hot! Use proper kitchen mitts or grabbers, be careful, and no touchy until they're cool enough.

So, let's get into this sterilization business like we mean it. Like scrubbing behind your ears serious. Like your bedroom is on a TV show serious. Like the fate of your delicious, canned masterpieces depends on it – because guess what? It does!

Finally, why all this focus on being clean? Because canning is about preserving not just food, but memories, too. When you pop open a jar of apple sauce, you want to remember the fun you had making it, not the time you had to toss a whole batch because it went bad.

Sterilization safeguards your hard work and those special moments, keeping them as fresh as the day you jarred them.

So get your game face on, canning champs. Be the boss of your kitchen with weapons of soap, water, and heat. Be a sterilization superhero, and those jars of deliciousness will be your victory trophies. Let's get canning, and let's do it the clean-way triumph!

Cautions and Tips for Kids

So you've just zipped through the exciting basics of canning and maybe you're itching to dive into the awesome world of jars, lids, and delicious preserves. Hold up! Before you turn the kitchen into your personal science lab, let's chat a few super important safety tips. Can-do? Yes, you can, but with a little know-how under your belt!

First, I've got to tell you, heat is a big deal in canning. And when I say big, I mean like, the kind of big where you want to make sure you're not treating the stove like your personal hand warmer. Always have an adult around when it's time to play with the heat. They're like your kitchen sidekick, keeping things safe while you focus on being the canning superhero you were born to be.

Now, remember the clean part? You're dealing with food that you want to stay yum for a long time. That means you can't let any pesky bacteria join your canning party. Wash your hands like you just finished finger painting and make sure all your tools, jars, and surfaces are superhero-level clean.

Speaking of germ-fighting, let's talk about the jars and lids. Those babies need to be as clean as a new whistle. That means boiling them or sticking them in hot, hot water before using them. It's like giving your jars a proper spa day before they get filled with deliciousness.

Getting handsy with food is super fun, but hot jam and splatter burns? Not so much. Did I hear oven mitts? Oh yeah, your hands' new best friends! Slip 'em on and keep those fingers looking just as fabulous as they are—no crispy fingertips allowed in this kitchen shindig.

Measure like a math whiz, but also like someone who knows that the wrong amount of sugar or pectin could turn your jams and jellies from fab to drab—or worse, unsafe. Stick to the script (recipe) with the focus of an astronaut on a space mission.

If sharp tools make you go, "Yikes!" then this tip's for you. Yes, cutting your fruits and veggies is part of the fun, but so is keeping all ten digits attached. Cut away from your body and take it slow—think of it as a peaceful Zen moment with peaches or a calm cucumber minute.

And about all that equipment... Pressure canners, boiling water canners, jar lifters – sounds like a sci-fi movie, but they're your trusty gear. Respect these tools—they're not toys. Use them with focus and always, I mean always, with an adult's help.

Heads up, my bubbling jar buddies! Things can get a little volcanic when your preserves are cooking. Bubble over? Yep, it happens. Keep a safe distance, like you would with an unknown species in the wild— observe, but don't get too close without taking precautions.

Bubbles aren't just in the pot, they're in jars too. We're not making soda here, so we've got to de-bubble the filled jars before sealing them, gently sliding a non-metallic utensil around the inside edge. It's like you're telling those air bubbles, "Party's over, pals!"

Let's get a bit sciency here for a sec: the timing is critical! When the instructions say process for X amount of time, they mean it. Not enough time and the bacteria are having a pool party; too much time and your food is on a one-way trip to Mushville. Stick to the time like glue—set a timer if you have to.

After the jar-jiving in the canner is done, they need some chill time, but not the fridge kind. Instead, they hang out on the counter, getting their cool back slowly. It's like after a monster game of tag—you can't just go zero to nap; you need to wind down.

Let's not forget labels. Tagging your jars with the contents and the date is like making a tiny time capsule. You'll thank yourself later when you're curiously eyeing a jar wondering, 'What in the world of wonders did I can last August?'

And you know what's really cool? Share the food love! But only after you're the master of the jar, confident in your sterilization groove, and have double-checked, maybe even triple-checked the safety steps. Share the tastiest, and safest, goodies on the block!

Finally, chill out and have some fun! Think of canning as your delicious diary of seasons and flavors. You're keeping the sun in a jar with all that summer fruit, and bottling the coziness of autumn with those apple preserves. It's like a high-five from Mother Nature herself!

Phew! Look at you, ready to conquer the kitchen with crafty care and charismatic canning charm. Stick to these tips like jam on toast, and you're all set to jam, pickle, and preserve your way into the canning hall of fame! Let's get those jars rockin' and rollin' to the rhythm of safety and fun!

Chapter 3:
Tools of the Trade

Now that we've tackled canning safety, let's dive into the crux of the matter—the magical wizardry of canning tools! Imagine you're a kitchen wizard, and every good wizard needs their wand and spellbook, right? In the mystical land of canning, these include your sturdy pot, trustworthy tongs, and shiny jars that hold untold delicious secrets. We're talking about the ensemble cast necessary to transform farm-fresh produce into shelf-stable treasures. No need for wand-waving, though, because these tools are very real and just waiting to get to work! We're not just popping tops off store-bought cans; we're the creators, the canners, the architects of apple butter and the engineers of strawberry jam! Sure, you could try canning with just any old kitchen gear, but that's like playing soccer with a basketball—it might work, but it's not quite right. So let's gear up with the right equipment to make canning a winning goal every time!

The Essential Canning Equipment

Just as a knight needs armor and a wizard requires a wand, you aspiring canning champions need the right gear to conquer the quest of jarring those scrumptious fruits and veggies! In our canning kingdom, the trusty tools aren't magical, but they're just as important. Picture a sturdy, lidded canning pot; it's like your cauldron for cooking up canning spells. Mason jars with seals and rings are your vessels for capturing and preserving the treasures of flavor. A jar lifter, that magical claw, keeps your fingers from a dance with dragons—uhh, I mean, from getting burned. Remember, an unsung hero of canning is the non-metallic spatula, great for stirring and releasing those pesky air bubbles that try to sneak in. And don't forget a clean kitchen towel, the trusty sidekick for wiping down jar rims. With these gadgets in your satchel, you'll be on your way to becoming the Merlin of marmalades and the Arthur of apple butter!

Optional Gadgets That Are Fun to Use

After mastering the basics, it's time to amp up your canning game with some fancy schmancy gadgets that might not be essential, but are definitely nifty to have around. They can make the whole canning process feel like a breeze and inject an extra dose of fun into your kitchen escapades!

Let's talk about the cherry pitter, my friends. If you've ever gotten yourself ready to can some delish cherries, you know the pit can be a, well, pitfall. It's small, it's sneaky, and it doesn't want to leave its cherry home. Enter the cherry pitter! It makes removing those little stony invaders a cinch, and trust me, your fingers will thank you for not staining them crimson red.

Now, for those of you with a palate that leans on the zesty side, a zest grater might just be your new best bud. Whether you're canning jams, marmalades, or anything that could use a splash of citrus sparkle, a zest grater will help you sprinkle that tangy magic without hauling out a bulky grater or getting the bitter pith involved.

How about dealing with pesky kernels when you're canning corn? I present to you: the corn stripper! Okay, it might sound silly, but this gadget is seriously cool. It strips those kernels right off the cob cleanly, so you can can that sweet, fresh corn goodness without any hassle or cob bits tagging along for the ride.

While we're on the topic of stripping (vegetables, people, vegetables), a good vegetable peeler can be a life-changer. You might think a basic peeler can do the job just fine, but there are peelers out there that can julienne your veggies for you! Yep, that means you can get fancy-looking veggies with minimal effort. How cool is that?

Let's get a little techy now and talk about a digital kitchen scale. Eyeballing ingredients can be risky business in the canning world. For recipes where precision matters, a digital kitchen scale will give you the exactness you need to ensure your efforts are not all for naught.

Jar lifters, while part of the 'essentials,' can come in many varieties. Some have a spring-loaded handle that makes lifting jars out of hot water as easy as pie. Speaking of pie, can you imagine canning your own homemade pie fillings? You'll feel like a canning wizard!

I know some of you out there have the artistic flair and creative spark. Well, have you ever heard of a canning funnel with headspace measurements? It not only helps you pour your scrumptious concoctions into jars without making a mess, but also allows you to measure the perfect amount of headspace. It's like having a little helper that ensures your canned treasures seal properly.

For the jam and jelly aficionados, behold the jelly strainer. No more fishing out fruit clumps unless you want them there! This little gizmo will help you achieve the smoothest, clearest jams or jellies you could wish for. It's like a magic wand for your fruit spread fantasies!

If you're canning stock or soup, consider getting your hands on a fat separator. A fat separator lets you pour out that rich stock while holding back the fat. You'll feel like a scientific kitchen genius watching the layers separate!

And who could forget the magnetic lid lifter? Nobody likes fishing around for lids in a pot of hot water. The magnetic lid lifter is like a magic wand that picks up your lids out of boiling water or sterilization baths so you can stay burn-free.

Feeling a bit fancy? How about a canning scoop with a curved edge that fits perfectly along the side and bottom of the pot? It lets you scoop out every last bit of your delicious creations with pinpoint precision, meaning no tasty morsel gets left behind.

Last but not least, get ready to meet the pressure canner's snazzy cousin—the electric pressure canner. It takes the guessing out of the process with presets for different foods. It's like upgrading from a bike to a sports car in the canning highway!

Of course, don't feel like you need to rush out and get all these gadgets at once. Canning is about patience, practice, and joy—and the best gadgets sometimes are the ones that simply make you smile with their cleverness. So, choose your tools wisely, and let them add a sprinkle of excitement to your canning journey! Who knows, one of these gadgets might just become the superhero sidekick in your canning stories.

As you contemplate introducing these optional gizmos into your canning routine, remember the key is to have fun and let creativity reign. These gadgets are meant to complement your skills, not complicate them. Keep experimenting, keep laughing at the spills, and whatever you do, keep on canning!

Chapter 4:
The Science of Canning

Cool your jets, my intrepid canners, as we now dive into the fascinating fizz and pop of *The Science of Canning*! Ever wonder what's really going on beneath those lids and within those jars as they bubble away in their hot water baths? Well, you're about to become a mini food scientist! It's all about locking in the yum and zapping the bad bugs that make food go "bleh!" - and that's no small feat. When we can, we're playing with time itself, pausing it, so that scrumptious strawberry jam or those perfectly pickled peppers can make it to your table months later, as fresh as the day they were sealed. Now, don't fret, we won't get too crazy with the chemistry sets; it's all about simple science magic. Like how heat slams the door on bacteria, or why acid is such a big deal in this can-land. By the end of this chapter, you'll get the hang of why we're so keen on keeping our food in tip-top shape and just how canning does the trick. So, let's simmer down and learn the whys, the hows, and the "a-ha's" of keeping your food safe, appetizing, and ready for your next adventure!

How Canning Preserves Food

Have you ever opened a can of peaches and found them just as tangy and sweet as a summer day, even in the middle of winter? That's the magic of canning! Essentially, canning is a super-heroic method of locking in freshness and flavor. Here's how it works: when food is packed into jars and heated, this clever process kicks out all the pesky bacteria and yeasts that usually cause food to spoil. It's kind of like closing all the doors to keep the cold out. The heating step also seals the lids tight, which makes sure no micro-invaders can sneak back in. Plus, without air inside, foods don't get the chance to oxidize and turn as brown as a bear in hibernation. So, fruits and veggies stay deliciously vibrant and nutrients aren't going on any adventures outside the jar. Remember, kids, canning isn't just about preserving food; it's about preserving taste, nutrients, and all those summer vibes any time of the year!

What Happens Inside the Jar? So, grab your magnifying glass, mini food scientists, because we're about to take a tiny journey into the fascinating world of a canning jar during the canning process. It's quite the party in there, and you're invited to sneak a peek!

First off, when we talk about canning, we're basically playing matchmaker between fresh food and jars. But what makes this a lasting relationship instead of a short fling? It's all about preservation, pals! Now, imagine a jar of raspberry jam. Those berries didn't just tumble into the jar willy-nilly. Oh no, they encountered some serious science!

When you heat the jam and pour it into jars, you're actually getting rid of unwanted guests at the party - like bacteria, yeasts, and molds. Heat is like the bouncer at the door, making sure only the good stuff stays. Then, when you seal the jar with a lid and the jar cools down, the seal acts like an exclusive VIP rope, not letting those uninvites back in.

Crucial to this is the vacuum effect which happens as the contents cool. Have you ever put a lid on a hot container and later found it hard to open because it's sealed tight? That's the vacuum pulling the lid down, sealing the show inside the jar.

Next up, innocent air hanging out inside the jar. When heated, this air wants to escape – and that's good because it helps create the vacuum. As the jar cools after processing, the air contracts and the pressure outside the jar becomes greater than the pressure inside. This is what makes that satisfying 'pop' sound as the lid seals – think of it as a high-five for doing a good job!

Now let's talk about the brine or syrup in pickles and canned fruits. These aren't just any tasty liquids; they're preservatives. Sugar syrup and vinegar brine are like secret agents. They make the environment inside the jar too tough for most bacteria to survive in, keeping your food safe and scrumptious.

Don't forget about acid, my friends. Many foods naturally high in acid are already tough terrains for bacteria. Add a little extra lemon juice or vinegar, and you've just turned the environment inside that jar into a fortress against spoilage.

Don't think the lid is just a pretty top piece – it's armed with a sealant that's heat-sensitive. Heating the jar makes this seal soft, allowing it to mold onto the jar's rim, creating an airtight seal as it cools. It's like when you make a clay sculpture, wet your fingers, and smooth out the edges to perfection.

In certain types of canning, like water bath canning, something super cool happens – 'thermal processing' is the technical term. This is the step where jars, filled with delicious things and capped with their lids, take a hot water dive. As the water heats, the contents of the jar expand, pushing more air out and further ensuring that perfect seal we talked about.

But what's the deal with canning things like beans or meats that don't get along well with just a water bath? Bring in the pressure canner, our mighty hero. It uses the power of steam and pressure to bring the temperature up higher than boiling water can – a must for these low-acid foods who need extra convincing to behave inside the jar.

The science of canning also helps retain flavors. By sealing everything up tight, you lock in the freshness and the taste. Imagine it like trapping all the fun of a summer day inside a jar – so when it's cold and grey outside, opening a jar of peaches is like your taste buds throwback to sunny picnics and running through sprinklers.

And here's a fun fact: sometimes there's a color change! It's nothing to worry about – it's just the natural reaction to heat and light. It's kind of like your jeans fading in the sun; they're still your cozy jeans, just a little lighter in color.

Texture changes can happen, too. That's because the heat during canning can break down fibers or firm up fruits or veggies in different ways. It's like how spaghetti is crunchy when uncooked but nice and tender when boiled. It's still delicious, just a bit different in the jar.

As for nutrition, canning is like putting a pause button on food. Most of the vitamins and minerals are preserved right there with the flavors. So, when you pop open that jar of green beans, you're releasing a mini-explosion of garden goodness.

Lastly, let's not forget the sugar and salt that are sometimes added. Besides adding flavor, they're sort of like the fortress guards, helping to keep food from spoiling. But they are also about balance - too much can overpower, and too little might not do the job. It's all about finding that sweet (or savory) spot for your preserved treats.

So, the next time you press your nose up against the glass and gaze into a canning jar, remember: there's a whirlwind of scientific wonder happening in there. Each jar of preserves is a tiny kingdom where the rules of keeping food safe and delicious reign supreme! And you, my dear young canners, are the master rulers of these glass-bound realms!

Chapter 5:
Starting Simple – Jams and Jellies

Just like a magician pulls a rabbit out of a hat, you're about to pull off something pretty amazing yourself – making your own jams and jellies! We've already learned the ropes of canning, made sure everything's squeaky clean, and got our tools ready. Now it's time to dive into the sweet, sticky world of spreads. If you think that strawberries and grapes are just for snack time, think again! These fruity wonders can transform, with a bit of sugar, heat, and pectin, into glistening jars of homemade goodness. You'll be stirring, tasting, and pouring like a pro. And the best part? There's no top hat or wand required, just your kitchen and some excited taste buds. So wash those fruits, cinch up your apron, and let's get ready to spread some joy – one spoonful of jam at a time!

Your First Canning Recipe

Now that we've got our canning safety badges on and learned about the quirky science behind preserving, it's time to dive into your very first canning recipe - drumroll, please - jam! Imagine the brightest, ripest berries you can think of, popping with color and flavor. We're going to transform them into a jam so fabulous, you might just want to eat it straight from the jar (but let's get it canned first!). We'll start with a classic berry jam, whisking together fruit and sugar and watching the magical dance as it thickens into spreadable sunshine. You'll learn the step-by-step process, from mashing those juicy berries to hearing the satisfying 'pop' of the jar sealing. Remember, it's like crafting a potion in a cauldron, but your kitchen is the laboratory, and your ingredients are the spell components. So grab a spoon – or better yet a ladle – and let's create some canning magic that would make even the most seasoned kitchen wizards proud!

Fruity Fun: Mix and Match Flavor Ideas Imagine a world where strawberries and kiwis are best pals, where peaches and raspberries share secret handshakes, and where apples and cinnamon stick together through thick and thin. Welcome to the adventurous land of mix-and-match fruit flavors in canning!

Let's start with the basics – berries. They're like the cool kids of the fruit world, and they love to mingle in jars. Combining blueberries, raspberries, and blackberries in a jam is not just a great idea; it's a berry bonanza! Each berry brings its unique zing to the party, and the result is a jam that's bursting with flavors and perfect for slathering on toast or dolloping on yogurt.

Ever think about inviting tropical fruits to your canning fiesta? Mango and pineapple are like the beach buddies of fruit flavors. Mixing these two creates a sunny, exotic jam that'll make your taste buds hula dance. And hey, why not toss in some coconut flakes for a little extra vacation vibe? It's all about creating a jar full of sunshine, no matter what the weather's like outside.

Let's not forget about the classic combo: apples and cinnamon. There's something about this duo that's just so right, like best friends that finish each other's sentences. When they come together in a spread, it's like warm apple pie without the crust — and who wouldn't want to dig into that?

For those who like to walk on the wild side, how about a zesty peach and ginger jam? The sweet peaches are like the laid-back friend that everyone loves, while ginger is the spicy one in the group who's always up for an adventure. When they team up, the result is a jam with a kick that'll wake up your morning toast.

Don't be afraid to mix different types of the same fruit, either. Combining sweet and tart cherries can make for a jam that has a full spectrum of cherry awesomeness. It's like a cherry party in a jar, and you're invited to spread the fun on everything!

Figs and oranges? Oh yes, let's go there. It's an unexpected match that creates a sophisticated and complex flavor profile. This combo is like the interesting new kid that everyone wants to know. It not only tastes great but is a sure-fire conversation starter at the breakfast table.

Love a good mystery? How about a mystery berry jam where you toss in a mix of whatever berries you have on hand? It's a thrilling fruit lottery in every jar. One spoonful might be all strawberry, and the next could be a berry explosion. It's exciting, unpredictable, and oh-so-delicious.

Here's one for the citrus lovers: orange and lemon marmalade. It's like sunshine and zest had a baby, and its name is Delicious. The sweet and tangy flavors of the oranges and lemons play off each other perfectly, creating a marmalade that's a bright start to the day.

Craving some nostalgia? Try a grape and vanilla bean jam. This blend is reminiscent of childhood but with a grown-up twist. The familiar grape flavor feels like a warm hug, while the vanilla adds a touch of elegance. It's comfort food in a jar.

Adventure is waiting in a pear and cranberry combo as well. The crisp sweetness of pears combined with the tart pop of cranberries creates a jam that's as beautiful in color as it is in taste. It's a jar full of fall flavors that you can enjoy any time of the year.

And who says you can't have dessert in a jam? A chocolate raspberry spread is a dream come true for those of us with a sweet tooth. The raspberries add a tangy freshness that cuts through the rich chocolate. Whether it's on pancakes or straight from the spoon, it's a decadent treat.

Feeling wild about watermelon? Try a watermelon and lime jam for a tropical twist. The melon's sweetness, combined with the lime's tangy zing, makes for a refreshing and unique flavor that will stand out on any pantry shelf.

What about the holidays? Cranberry and orange jam captures the essence of the season. The tartness of cranberries mingles with the sweetness of oranges to make a spread that tastes like the holidays in a jar. It's the perfect homemade gift that screams "I'm tasty and thoughtful."

And let's not leave out a bit of heat – a strawberry jalapeño jam could be just the thing to spice things up. The strawberries bring sweetness to the table, while the jalapeños throw in a little fire. It's a bold move for a jam, but you're a daring canning artist, aren't you?

Finally, if you can't decide on one flavor, create a fruit salad jam. Toss in whatever fruits are in season – peaches, plums, berries – and make a jam that's like a party in a jar. Every bite is a delicious surprise, and it's a great way to celebrate the bounty of the season.

These mix and match flavor ideas are just the beginning. Let your creative juices flow, and don't be afraid to try something new. Who knows? You might just invent the next great jam sensation. Happy mixing, matching, and canning, my fruity friends!

Chapter 6:
Pickles and Relishes – The Tangy Treats

After spreading your jam on a fresh piece of toast, it's time we switched gears and dived into a world where the pucker power of vinegar rules! That's right, we're wading into the tangy waters of making pickles and relishes. Imagine being able to pull out a crunchy pickle or a zesty relish at your next barbecue that you made yourself! Nothing beats that homemade crunch, and in this chapter, we're all about transforming cucumbers and veggies into jars of joy that pack a punch. And it isn't just cucumbers that get to have all the fun; we'll be exploring all sorts of vegetables that you can turn into sour sensations. You'll get to know the basics of the pickling process, how to safely play with flavors, and even toss in some surprising twists like sweet pickles or fiery spikes of chili. So, grab your favorite veggies and let's get pickling – it's gonna be a flavor-packed ride!

The Basics of Pickling

After you've gotten the lowdown on jams and jellies, it's time to tickle your taste buds with the zesty world of pickles! Think of pickling as a kitchen magic trick where vinegar, water, and salt transform cucumbers into crunchy, delightful dills. But hey, don't stop there! Anything from carrots to cauliflower can take a dive into this tangy bath. This transformation is all thanks to the amazing process of fermentation and acidification, which not only creates that mouth-puckering flavor but also acts as the ultimate food preserver. And the best part? It's so simple, it's almost silly. Just whisk together a briny potion, immerse the veggies, and watch as they become the stars of the snack world. Get ready to create jars filled with zing and zip that'll light up your fridge and your palate!

Customizing Your Crunch Picking up our tangy adventure from where we left off, it's time to dive into the world of making those pickles pop with personality. Because let's face it, a crunch can be cool, classic, or crazy—depending on how you spin it. And that's exactly what we're going to do: spin that pickle jar into your very own carnival of flavor.

First things first, grab your notepad because creativity doesn't start until we put down some ground rules. You're probably wondering, "What's the first step to becoming a pickle Picasso?" It's simple: know thy pickle. Understand the basic pickling solution—vinegar, water, and salt—and you've got your canvas ready for the magic to happen.

So, vinegar is your tart taste-maker, but she's also a bit of a blank slate, ready to soak up whatever amazing tastes you introduce her to. Get creative! Apple cider vinegar will give your pickles a fruity note, while white vinegar provides a clean, sharp taste. Imagine painting with flavors, and your taste buds are the canvas!

Toss in those spices like you're sprinkling fairy dust. Each little bit changes the flavor. Dill is, of course, the quintessential pickle partner, but why stop there? Mustard seeds can add a nice little kick, while peppercorns can give a gentle heat that'll have you feeling like you've got a cozy fireplace in your mouth.

Now brace yourselves for the next big thing: the sweet twist. Add a pinch (or a handful, we won't judge) of sugar to your brine, and watch your pickles go from wallflower to disco queen. We're talking about a sweet-and-sour sensation that'll have your tongue dancing in no time.

Consider also the crunch itself. How firm do you want your pickles to be? Alum can be a friend here, giving your pickles a firmer texture, but don't worry if you can't find it—the freshness of the cucumbers and the length of the pickling time are also key crunch factors.

Let's not forget about the fun of adding other veggies. A slice of onion, a wedge of bell pepper, or even a clove of garlic can make your pickle jar a treasure chest of tastes. Mix and match different vegetables to see how they complement each other and bring out new flavors in your pickles.

Sweet on heat? Spice it up! A chili pepper or a dash of hot sauce in the mix can turn up the temperature on your pickle production. But remember, the longer the brine sits, the hotter it gets, so experiment with timing to get that heat just right.

And speaking of time, it's not just a watch thing—it's a pickle thing too! The longer your cucumbers bathe in that brine, the more intense the flavor. Sometimes a quick pickle is all you need for a snack, while other times, you'll want those cucumbers to swim around and soak up all that goodness for a week or more.

But let's circle back to our veggie friends. Remember, you can pickle more than just cucumbers! Carrots, green beans, and even okra can join the pool party. Just imagine opening a jar of your very own veggie medley— it's like a garden party in your mouth!

Another pro tip: Use your leftover pickle brine to give a second life to other veggies. It's like the encore at a concert, except with pickles. Once your original batch is gone, throw in some fresh veggies and wait for the magic to happen again. Thrifty and nifty!

For those who want to walk on the wild side of flavor, get funky with the fermentation. Lacto-fermented pickles switch up the process, using saltwater and natural bacteria to bring the flavor. It's a different kind of sour—complex and riveting. A bit like jazz in a jar.

And don't forget the look of your jar. A colorful mix of vegetables can be just as much a feast for the eyes as for the taste buds. Place the ingredients intentionally and watch as your pickle jar becomes a stained-glass window of deliciousness.

Gather your friends and family for a pickling party. Everyone can bring their unique ingredients, and together, you'll make a symphony of pickled goodness. Plus, it's way more fun to share your custom flavors with others. It might even spark a bit of friendly competition—who will be the pickling champion?

So there you have it, mini-chefs and canning comrades! You're well on your way to becoming a master of the custom crunch. Whether you're a fan of sweet, spicy, or somewhere in between, your pickles can be as unique as you are. Put on that apron, roll up those sleeves, and let's make a pickle jar that's packed with personality!

Chapter 7:
Canning Vegetables and Soups

Just when you've mastered the art of transforming berries into jam, it's time to roll up your sleeves because we're diving into the world of canning vegetables and soups. Imagine opening up a jar of garden-fresh carrots in the middle of winter or savoring a bowl of home-canned minestrone on a chilly evening! Vegetables and soups can be a bit tricky because they're usually low in acid, but have no fear – with a few simple tips, you'll be safely canning these goodies like a pro. We'll uncover the secrets of packing veggies so they stay crisp and delicious, and I'll walk you through how to turn your favorite soup recipes into shelf-stable meals you can enjoy any time. Get your soup pots and canning jars ready – it's time to preserve the bounty of the earth!

Veggie Adventures in a Jar

After mastering the basics of jammin' with fruits and getting pickled with cucumbers, it's time to amp up your canning game to the hearty world of veggies! Imagine opening your pantry to find a rainbow of jars filled with snappy green beans, sweet corn, and even some sassy salsa verde you whipped up last summer. That's right, with a pinch of patience and a dash of daring, you can transform those garden-fresh veggies into year-round treasures. No magic needed, just a little can-do attitude and you'll be stacking your shelves with homemade veggie delights that'll make your taste buds do a happy dance. Trust me, once you pop the lid on your own batch of canned carrots or zesty zucchini, you'll feel like a kitchen wizard—and who doesn't want to be a wizard, right? So let's get those pots bubbling and jars burping because we're about to preserve some vegetable awesomeness!

Soup's On: Canning Your Favorite Comfort Foods

Let's get cozy with cans! We've talked veggies, and now it's time to ladle out the love for soups in jars. Imagine having your ultimate comfort food ready to go at any time, preserved perfectly for that rainy day. That's what we're stirring up in this chapter!

First off, let's chat about why canning soups is such a cool idea. Soup is like a warm hug in a bowl, right? It soothes, it comforts, and, guess what, it can be packed with nutritious yumminess. When you can your favorite soup, you capture that hug and keep it on your shelf, ready when you need that warm embrace of flavors.

But hold on, before you start throwing everything but the kitchen sink into your soup pot, let's talk recipes. Soup recipes need a little tweaking before they're ready to be sealed away in jars. This is because some ingredients are home-canning divas and others… not so much. For example, noodles and rice can get mushy, and dairy tends to be a no-go as it can separate and spoil. Stick to the good stuff like vegetables, beans, and meats that hold up to the heat.

Creating your own magic potion of soup starts with a solid base – and that's usually a broth or stock. Chicken, beef, vegetable, or even the mysterious bone broth – pick your potion. Just make sure it's tasty and clear of fats that could spoil your hard work. Skim off any scum and fat after boiling your bones or veggies – you want a pure elixir!

Chopping up all those veggies and other goodies can be a great way to get the whole family involved. Kiddos can learn cutting skills (with close supervision and safe tools, of course) and they'll feel super proud seeing their handiwork in those shiny jars. Always remember that uniform pieces not only look neat but also help ensure everything cooks properly.

Now let's talk spices – they're the secret whispers of flavor that can make or break a soup. Some spices get stronger over time, and some fade away. Go easy on them when prepping your soup for canning. You can always add more zing when you open the jar and heat up the soup for eating.

Canning soups is a bit different from jams or pickles because you usually have to use a pressure canner. This gizmo is like the superhero of canners, using pressure and steam to zap any bacteria so that your soup stays safe and delicious for months. If you've never used one, no worries, it's not as intimidating as it seems. Just follow the instructions and you'll be a pressure canning champ in no time!

Once your soups are bubbling away in the pressure canner, use that waiting time to daydream about all the amazing meals you're prepping in advance. Imagine coming home from a long day of school or play, and instead of waiting for dinner, your homemade soup is just a jar lid away. Just heat and eat!

Let's not forget about those secret ingredients that give soups a special homemade touch. Maybe it's a bay leaf or a spring of fresh thyme. These are the delightful details that will make your soup taste like it's fresh out of the pot every time.

Soups are seriously awesome for sharing, too. Think about it: making a big batch doesn't take much more time than a small one. And who wouldn't love getting a jar of homemade soup as a gift? It's like handing someone a ready-to-enjoy meal that's full of comfort and care.

After your jars have cooled down, make sure to check the seals – this is crucial to keeping your soup safe. You're looking for lids that are tight and don't pop when you press them. A good seal means you've nailed it, and that soup is set for the shelf life it deserves.

Labeling your jars might not seem like a thrilling step, but trust me, six months down the line when you're trying to figure out if it's tomato basil or pumpkin squash soup – you'll be thankful for a label.

Plus, decorating labels can be a blast and add a personalized touch to your pantry!

If you've followed all the steps and safety tips, your soup will be waiting for you whenever you're craving that cozy, comforting goodness. It's like having a secret stash of culinary contentment lined up on your shelf. No need to fret about what's for dinner; your previous cooking-self has already got you covered.

In closing this steamy section on soups, remember that canning is not just about preserving food, but also the warm and fuzzy feelings that come with homemade goodness. Your souped-up jars are time capsules of care, ready to be reopened and enjoyed whenever you need a pick-me-up.

Sharing your canned soups can also warm hearts and bellies beyond your home. It's an act of love and generosity to pass on a jar of your home-cooked specialty. So, let's fill those jars and spread the joy of soup – one can at a time!

And just like that, we've ladled out plenty of tips and stirred in some fun for canning those favorite comfort foods. Keep that can-do attitude simmering, because up next, we're diving into the fruity world of canning whole fruits!

Chapter 8:
Fruity Fun – Canning Whole Fruits

So now you've jammed with jams and pickled with the best, but are you ready to tackle the titan of the fruit world? That's right – we're taking a whole new bite out of canning by preserving whole fruits! Picture this: the dead of winter, but your pantry is like a secret garden bursting with jars of summer-perfect peaches, peerless pears, and cherries that'll make you, well, cherry! In Chapter 8, we're diving into the world of canning whole fruits without losing their shape or that just-picked flavor. It's like putting nature's candy in your cupboard! Get ready to learn the ins and outs of packing fruit in jars – we'll talk about picking the best fruits for canning, the methods to keep 'em whole, and how to keep things sweet (or tart, if that's how you roll) without having to worry about any funky additives. Canning whole fruits is not just preserving food; it's like bottling up a little jar of sunshine. So, let's get the cans rolling and the fruits flying in for a wholesomely good time!

Peaches, Pears, and More

After you've jammed and jellied, it's time to level up your canning game with some whole fruit fun! Peaches and pears are the crown jewels of canned treasures you can stash away in your pantry, and guess what? They're just the starting line-up. There's a whole roster of fruits waiting to dive into those jars, like plums, apricots, and cherries. And here's a juicy secret: with the right steps, you'll lock in that just-picked taste that explodes in your mouth months later. Now, don't worry about wrinkling your nose over any fuzzy peach skin; we'll get to how you can slip those right off. Plus, there's nothing quite like the 'oohs' and 'ahs' you'll get when you pop open a jar of whole fruits you canned yourself. They're not just tasty; they look like a jar full of edible gems. So, grab your favorite fruits, roll up your sleeves, and let's get those fruits swimming in their syrupy pools. They can't wait to take the plunge!

Syrups and Seasonings to Spice It Up

Okay, jam masters, pickle pros, and canning commanders! You've learned the basics of throwing fruits and veggies into jars and making sure they're snug as a bug. But now it's time to go from "good" to "goodness gracious, that's amazing!" with syrups and seasonings. Imagine biting into a peach so divine you think you've teleported to a sunny orchard, or a pear so perfectly spiced, it dances the cha-cha with your taste buds. That's what we're aiming for. Let's get mixing!

First up, we're talking syrups. Syrups aren't just sugary water; they're the cozy sweaters for your fruits, the ultimate hug that keeps them juicy and joyous in their glassy homes. You can start with the simple syrup – just water and sugar, friends – but here's where the seasoning samba begins.

Grab cinnamon sticks, vanilla pods, or even a few shavings of nutmeg. Drop them into your syrup and what do you have? A concoction that will make your canned fruits sing an opera of flavors. Your kitchen's gonna smell so good, don't be surprised if the neighbors come knocking!

But wait, there's more. You can't talk about flavoring without hollering for herbs. Mint, rosemary, or basil can join your syrup, and they aren't just there to look pretty. These green guys pack a punch that can elevate your peach preserves or berry bonanza into something your taste buds won't forget.

And let's not forget our zesty assistants - citrus peels! A strip of lemon, lime, or orange peel can hang out in your syrup, too. It's like inviting a little sunshine into each jar. Just remember, these party guests don't like to overstay – be sure to remove the peels after boiling the syrup to avoid bitterness.

Cloves and allspice berries are keeping it cool on the spice rack, but invite them in! They're tiny, but boy do they bring the zest to your zest. A couple of these buddies, and you'll have a fruity concoction that can stand up to any store-bought jar with a twinkle in its lid.

Moving onto sweet seasonings, and I'm not just talking sugar. Have you met honey? It's liquid gold, and it can get along with just about every fruit in the jar. Drizzle some in your syrup, and you've got yourself a natural sweetener that's buzzing with awesomeness.

Now, ever lay your eyes on maple syrup? This tree sap is not just for pancakes, pals. It has a way of holding hands with fruits like apples and pears and skipping down Flavor Lane in perfect harmony.

But don't just stop at sweet. Kick it up a notch with spices like ginger or cardamom. These aren't your typical seasoning soldiers; they bring warmth and a snappy zing that can make the difference between "yum" and "YUMMM!"

Sweetie pies, we must also chat about the power of fruit zest. A little rub-a-dub of lemon zest on sugar, left to mingle, creates this zingy sugar that's out of this world. Sprinkle that in your syrups or directly on the fruits before canning, and you've added a secret zappy flavor weapon.

Now, can we talk sauce? You've got your syrups down, but if you want to swim in deeper waters, let's bring in the sauce. A thick, velvety sauce cuddling up to your fruits is like the snuggliest blanket on a chilly night. And that's where spices like star anise can steal the show, turning your regular sauce into an enigmatic embrace of flavors.

Pssst, hot tip here: balance is the key. Don't throw the whole spice rack in at once. It's a symphony, not a scream-fest. Each note of flavor must have its solo, its time to shine, so your taste buds can appreciate the full melody of tastes.

Canning aficionados, remember, it's a tasting journey. Don't be afraid to play and discover. Maybe that odd-sounding strawberry and basil jam or that daring tomato and cinnamon sauce is your ticket to the canning hall of fame!

Finally, let's talk labels – because when you've crafted the Mona Lisa of syrups, you better believe it deserves a name tag. Scribble down not only the ingredients but also the love and care you sprinkled in. Give your creation a title that sings of the adventures within. "Grandma's Apple Pie in a Jar"? Oh, you betcha!

And there you have it – your fruit's new best buds, syrups and seasonings that will make those jars shelf superstars. Get creative, have fun, and remember, the greatest kitchen magician is the one who dares to sprinkle, stir, and savor the unexpected. Happy flavor forging, champions of cans!

Chapter 9:
Tomatoes, Salsas, and Sauces

Just when you think you've mastered the jammy, pickle-y world of canning, hold onto your hats—it's time to dive into the vibrant universe of tomatoes, salsas, and sauces! Think of tomatoes as your new best buds in the canning playground. These versatile fruits (yep, they're not veggies) are the superheroes of the canning world, morphing into anything from a chunky salsa that'll have your taste buds dancing, to a smooth sauce that can hug a plate of spaghetti like a warm, Italian embrace. And the best part? You're the maestro of flavor, conducting an orchestra of herbs, spices, and secret ingredients. Get ready to crush, dice, and simmer your way to canning stardom. Don't be shy—slather on that apron, rally your jars, and let's turn up the heat on sustainable snacking with some homemade goodness that'll make store-bought versions blush with envy!

The World of Canning Tomatoes

Imagine grabbing a sun-kissed tomato, ripe and beaming with flavor, and tucking its vibrant essence into a jar to savor year-round—now that's the magic of canning! Tomatoes are like the rock stars of the canning world; whether they're bopping around as cheerful cherry types or strutting their stuff as plump heirlooms, they are ready to jam (or should we say jell?) with you in the kitchen. When we embark on the tomato canning extravaganza, we're not just squishing fruits into jars; we're artisans painting with flavors and textures, preserving the summer's blush well into winter's chill. Peeling, squashing, seasoning—every step is a dance, every jar a trophy of our kitchen conquests. But wait, there's more! This is your chance to become a tomato whisperer, turning each bulbous beauty into tangy sauces, fiery salsas, or that perfect pizza topping. So, grab those jars, rev up the stove, and let's prove that whilst superheroes might not always wear capes, they certainly can wield a canning spoon like nobody's business!

Creating Salsas and Sauces from Scratch – who knew that playing with your food could be so much fun? And no, we're not talking about launching peas with your spoon like little green rockets. We're talking about mastering the craft of making your very own salsas and sauces and then canning them to enjoy all year round!

First things first, when you're making salsa or sauce from scratch, you're like a flavor wizard—mixing, matching, and conjuring up delicious tastes. But even the most powerful wizards need to start with the basics: tomatoes. Most salsas and sauces begin with these ruby-red gems. The best part? Tomatoes can taste super different depending on how you treat them. Roast them for a smoky kick, or keep them fresh for a salsa that's bright and zingy!

Now, it's time to choose your co-stars. Salsas and sauces are all about balance and harmony, so think about which flavors play well together. Want a salsa with a sweet twist? Try adding some juicy pineapple or mango. If it's sauce you're after, herbs like basil and oregano can turn it into a fragrant masterpiece.

Once you've picked your pals, it's chopping time! But keep your digits safe—knives are sharp, and we want the tomatoes diced, not your fingers. Chop everything into your desired size; chunky for salsas, smooth for sauces. Remember, texture is just as important as taste. It's what makes your mouth go, "Wow, I gotta have another scoop of that!"

Now comes the heat. If you're making sauce, get those tomatoes and their friends simmering on the stove. A long, slow cook will make everyone get along in the pot. For salsa, decide if you want it cooked or fresh. If you're cooking it, just a quick dance in the heat will do, enough to let the flavors mingle like guests at a dance party.

Herbs and spices are like magic dust for your creations. They can transport you around the world with just a sprinkle. Add some cumin and cilantro, and you're in Mexico! Some basil and thyme? Hello, Italy! But here's a little secret: always add a bit less than you think you need. You can always throw more in, but you can't take it out once it's in there.

You might want to crank up the zesty volume with some lemon or lime juice. Not only do they add pizzazz to the taste, but they also add acidity, which is super-duper important for canning safely—more on that later.

Why not throw in a curveball and add some secret ingredients? We're talking a spoonful of honey for sweetness, a dash of Worcestershire sauce for depth, or, if you're feeling brave, a slice of jalapeño for some heat. Just make sure you can handle the spice. No one wants a salsa that makes you drink a gallon of milk!

With your salsa or sauce taste-tested (the best part!) and perfected, it's canning time. This is when the freshly made creation gets tucked into jars like little kids into bed. Just as you'd read a bedtime story, be sure everything is clean and cozy. Sterilize your jars and lids, because germs trying to crash the canning party are a big no-no.

When filling those jars, leave a little space at the top—it's called "headspace," and it's vital for a good seal. It's like when you don't fill a bathtub all the way up, so you don't make a mini flood when you jump in.

Next, you'll process your jars. This means giving them a hot water bath or using a pressure canner, depending on what you're canning. Think of it as a spa day for your salsa or sauce. This step makes sure everything will be shelf-stable and ready to impress your taste buds months from now.

After processing, the jars need to chill out and relax. Let them sit without bumping or moving them around. You'll hear the glorious "pop" sound of jars sealing—music to a canner's ears! It's like hearing the buzzer when you win a basketball game. You did it!

If you've been patient and done everything right, your jars should now be sealed tight, ready to be labeled and stored. It's important to write down what's in the jar and when you made it because nobody likes a mystery jar in the pantry. Plus, you'll want to brag about that mouthwatering salsa you made in the summer during the chilly winter!

Before we wrap up our salsa and sauce saga, let's remember that safety comes first. Keep your kitchen clean, always follow the recipes and processing times, and you'll be a safe and savvy canner. It's kind of like following the rules of the road; it keeps everyone happy and healthy.

Creating your own salsas and sauces can be a ticket to flavor town and a great way to impress your family and friends with your culinary wizardry. Plus, you'll be eating something you made from scratch, which is extra tasty because it's spiced with your hard work and creativity. So go ahead, grab those tomatoes, heat up those jars, and remember: you're not just making food, you're making memories!

Chapter 10:
Creative Cans – Unique Ideas and Recipes

Okay, you've squished fruit into jams, crunched cucumbers into pickles, and you're pretty much a wizard when it comes to whipping up a tomato sauce that could make a grown-up cry tears of joy. Now let's turn up the fun dial to eleven with Chapter 10! Ever thought about infusing your own oils or making a jelly that tastes like your favorite candy? We've got a treasure trove of zany ideas that'll have your taste buds doing backflips. Just when you thought your canning skills were top-notch, we're about to make them legendary! We're not just putting food in jars – we're capturing magic. Get ready to twist traditional recipes and embark on a culinary craft adventure that could make your snacks the talk of the town and your meals a moment to remember. And who knows? Your masterpieces might just be the perfect gifts to spread the love. So, grab your favorite spoon, put on your creative chef's hat, and let's make some canning masterpieces!

Infusions and Flavored Oils

After acing your jams and mastering the pickle crunch, you're ready to dip your spoon into something slick and snazzy! It's time to dive into the world of infusions and flavored oils. Imagine drizzling a pizza with garlic-rosemary oil or jazzing up your salad with a raspberry-basil infusion. Sounds pretty chef-y, right? Well, you can! We're talking about oils that pack a punch with every drop and infusions that'll make your taste buds do a happy dance. They're sort of like the secret agents of flavor - a little goes a long way! And the best part? You get to be the kitchen wizard, mixing herbs, spices, fruits, or even chili peppers with oils and vinegars to create concoctions that are seriously next-level. So grab those jars, pick your potion of flavors, and let's get infusing! Just ensure you're super careful with cleanliness and storage because we want our food flavorful, not feisty with unwanted microbes!

Giving Canned Goods as Gifts

So you've graduated from just making jams and pickles for the pantry and now you're eyeing that teeming row of vibrant jars wondering, "Could these be the next great gift for grandma, or a super surprise for my BFF?" Spoiler alert: Yes, they can! Canned goods, made by your own two hands or four if you've teamed up with a pal, make wonderful and thoughtful gifts that bring a taste of homey goodness to any occasion.

You might be thinking, "But are my peach preserves posh enough for a present?" Let me tell you, nothing spells 'you're peachy keen in my book' quite like a jar of homemade peach preserves. Canned gifts are not just delicious; they're personal. Each jar is a little time capsule of your effort, care, and creativity. The best part? You can jazz them up with decorations, tags, or a cute ribbon to take them from pantry-grade to gift-glam in no time.

We've all been through the holiday drill: a mad dash to the store, followed by a frenzied flurry of gift wrapping. But imagine sidestepping that rigmarole by having gifts ready to go on your shelf. That's right, with home-canned goodies, you're always prepared for birthdays, holidays, and just-because days. As eco-warriors and penny-savers, we can't help but love a gift that's as sustainable as it is scrumdiddlyumptious.

Though, hold your horses if you think you're limited to the classics. Sure, strawberry jam is an old-time favorite, but the world of canning is your oyster (disclaimer: please don't can oysters without proper guidance). From spicy salsas to sumptuous syrups, there's a spectrum of deliciousness waiting to be bottled and bowed as presents. Think outside the jar!

Let's focus on making those jars look the part. A well-dressed jar goes from kitchen counter to gifting wonder with a few simple touches. It's like picking out the perfect outfit – but for your preserves. Grab a fabric scrap to cover the lid, a little twine for added rustic charm, or a bright label for a splash of fun. Now, your usual Tuesday night canned applesauce is donning its Sunday best.

And let's not forget the recipe card. Sharing the secret to your superb spaghetti sauce or the method behind your magical marmalade creates a gift that keeps on giving. It's like saying, "Here's a spoonful of love, and guess what? You can stir up your own whenever you like!" Now, doesn't that warm the cockles of your heart?

Okay, you've got your jars dressed up and ready to strut their stuff, but what about the hand-off? Whether it's a holiday exchange or a neighborly nod of appreciation, present your canned goods with the spirit they deserve. A genuine smile and a "Made this with you in mind" do more than any wrapping paper ever could.

Special days call for special gifts, and canning doesn't shy away from the challenge. Valentine's Day? How about a jar of cherry chutney with a 'Cherry-ish You' tag. Thanksgiving? A quart of crispy pickles might just get you a seat at the adult table. Homemade gifts for the win!

But it goes beyond playing dress-up or scribbling clever puns. Your canned gifts can tell a story, create a memory, or simply show someone that they're in your thoughts. Whether it's jam from berries you both picked last summer, or pickle brine reminiscent of grandma's recipe, it's about sharing a piece of a story, a place, a moment in time.

Remember, the best presents aren't always the shiniest or the most expensive. Sometimes, they're the ones that are packed with care and burst with the flavors of friendship and family. They are the ones that whisper (or if it's a particularly zesty salsa, shout), "You're special, and I took the time to make something unique just for you."

So next time you're considering what to give for that upcoming celebration, take a peek in your pantry. Those shelves might just hold the perfect present—a jar of your lovingly canned creations. And trust us, that's a gift sure to be remembered much longer than the lifespan of your average, run-of-the-mill knick-knack.

But enough of the chitchat – let's get canning! Remember, the best gifts are the ones that resonate with the receiver's taste buds and tug at their heartstrings. Whether it's a soothing soup for a friend in need or a zippy zest for your zestful cousin, let's make your jar be the one that breaks the mold (the good, kinda mold, not the icky kind).

Congratulations, you're now a master of giving from the heart... and the kitchen! Now go forth, my fellow canners, and spread the joy one jar at a time. Here's to gifts that are not canned, but canny—clever, creative, and cooked up with love.

And remember, with each jar you give away, you're not just spreading flavors—you're spreading happiness. Because in the end, isn't that what giving is all about?

From Garden to Jar

Have you ever wondered how that plump, juicy tomato from the garden transforms into the tangy marinara sauce atop your spaghetti? Or how crunchy cucumbers become zesty pickles in a sandwich? Well, it all starts with a seed—literally! In Chapter 11, we'll dig into the fabulous journey of growing your own canning ingredients. Imagine the satisfaction of watching your carrots, beans, and berries grow from tiny seeds to ripe, delicious produce that you can harvest with your own hands. But it's not just about the harvest; it's about turning that harvest into jars of scrumptious, shelf-stable delights. We'll explore how to transition smoothly from garden gloves to canning aprons, and why this cycle isn't just cool—it's ultra-sustainable. You won't just be a canning champ; you'll be a gardening guru too, creating what you can, and canning what you create!

Grow Your Canning Ingredients

Get ready to dive, shovel-first, into the magical world of growing your own canning ingredients! Imagine, tiny seeds blossoming into crispy cucumbers, plump tomatoes, and fragrant herbs, all ready to be transformed into jars of deliciousness that'll make your taste buds dance. Now, you don't need a green thumb to join this garden party— just a dash of curiosity and the willingness to get a bit muddy. Growing your veggies and fruits isn't just a way to make your canned creations taste better, it's like a secret ingredient for the soul, giving you the superpower to literally 'eat your garden.' You'll learn how the care you give to your plant pals pays off in a cornucopia of colors and flavors, which makes canning your harvest not just smart, but also incredibly satisfying. So, let's plant the seeds of tomorrow's scrumptious snacks today!

The Cycle of Sustainable Living - Ah, so we've scooped up some understanding about growing our own canning ingredients, and now we're plunging into the delightful world of sustainable living. Ever wonder how we can keep this beautiful planet of ours spinning happily with fresh air, lush gardens, and clean water? Living sustainably is like being part of a superhero squad - where every day is an opportunity to save the world, can by can!

Living sustainably means thinking about the big picture while doing little things every day. It's like a circle, where everything you do cycles back in amazing ways. When we talk about canning, we're not just filling jars – we're reducing waste, saving energy, and giving the supermarket a miss for once!

Picture this: you plant a tiny seed, give it some love and water, and boom! It's a tomato plant with more tomatoes than you know what to do with. Instead of saying "Oh my veggies!" you get to canning. And just like that, you've kicked the canning cycle into gear.

Why toss leftovers when they can become tomorrow's tomato sauce? By canning, you're a recycling rockstar. No mysterious ingredients or preservatives – it's all good, clean fun, and you know exactly what's going in those jars. And when you crack one open? It's like tasting sunshine in the middle of winter!

Oh, and let's chat Earth-friendliness for a hot sec. No need for a fridge means you're not just saving greenbacks, you're saving the big blue marble we call home. Less energy used equals more high-fives from Mother Nature.

But wait! Before those jars become part of a pantry constellation, think about scraps. Carrot tops, potato skins, all the bits normally tossed into the trash - why not start a compost heap? It's like a VIP club for leftovers where the only rule is 'decompose'. That heap will turn into gold – not real gold (we wish!), but compost that makes your garden go "Wow!" and "Thanks!"

Sharing is part of this cycle, too. That jam you made? It can cheer up your neighbor, or become the star at a school fundraiser. It's spreading love, one spoonful at a time, strengthening friendships, and even maybe making new pals. The gift of sustenance – there's nothing sweeter!

Get this, every jar you don't buy from the store is a pat on the back for your local wildlife. Fewer trucks on the roads, less air pollution, and happier squirrels (and who doesn't want happier squirrels?).

Let's talk water. Gardening can be thirsty work for the planet. But with rain barrels and smart watering ways, every drop counts. Collect rainwater and watch your garden gulp it up with joy – it's nature's own refreshment, no filter required!

Tallying up all the yums you've preserved? Don't fly past the labels. Use that imagination and jazz 'em up! But keep it green – think recycled paper or reusable tags. Make 'em bright, make 'em fun, and make sure they'll break down or can come back for an encore when your jar's empty.

Sustainable living also comes down to choices. Opt for local produce groups or farmers' markets. You can find organic wonders that practically jump into your jars, begging to be preserved. It's like joining a foodie club, where every member is as pumped about canning as you are.

If you feel like you've nailed this process, why not teach it? Pass the baton to pals or kiddos, so they, too, can join the sustainable brigade. This cycle continues, one person at a time, spreading the can-do attitude like wildflowers.

Remember, the jars you use are heroes in their own right – tough, reusable, and dependable, these glass sidekicks can be filled over and over. They're the quiet champions of sustainability, and guess what? They don't mind a bit.

And when your canning journey seems to wrap up at the end of the season, think again, buddy! Those empty jars are perfect for storing seeds for the coming year. That's right, pumpkin seeds today – pumpkin pie filling tomorrow. It's the circle of life, can-style.

Lastly, know that each little choice you make adds up. Choosing to can and preserve at home might feel small, but it's part of a bigger effort. Like ants building a colossal ant hill – it's teamwork where you, your family, and friends are all in it together, crafting a sustainable future one jar, one seed, and one delicious bite at a time.

So keep it up, amazing humans! Each jar you seal is a victory for our planet. Take pride in being part of the cycle of sustainable living. You're not just making food – you're making a difference. And hey, that's something worth celebrating, maybe with a slice of home-canned peach pie!

Chapter 12:
Community Canning – Sharing the Fun

Just when you thought canning couldn't get any cooler, we're about to turn up the heat with a whole chapter dedicated to canning with friends, family, and your awesome neighbors! Think of canning as the ultimate kitchen party—you're not just jarring tomatoes or pickling cucumbers, you're making memories and some rocking good recipes to boot. Picture this: tables lined with colorful fruits and veggies, jars clinking, and the sweet smell of simmering strawberry jam—pretty fantastic, right? Now imagine that with all your pals around, swapping stories, laughs, and maybe even creating a little friendly competition over who can come up with the zingiest pickle. It's not just about filling your pantry; it's about filling your life with good company and the warm fuzzies that come from sharing the art of canning. By the end of this chapter, you'll be a community canning crusader, ready to spread the word that when it comes to canning, more is merrier, healthier, and a whole lot of fun!

Hosting Canning Parties and Classes

Imagine turning your kitchen into a bustling hub of giggles and clinking jars—that's right, it's party time, but with a twist! Hosting canning parties and classes is all about mixing the fun of a get-together with the thrill of creating delicious jams, pickles, and preserves by yourself, but with the energy of your friends or classmates. It's like the ultimate craft day, except you get to eat your creations! You'll need a few extra pots and some aprons to keep things tidy, but the main ingredient is teamwork. Gather a group of pals, family members, or even your scout troop, and dive into the colorful world of peaches, plums, and peppers—everyone can choose their favorite! Not only is it a great way to spend an afternoon, but you'll be teaching everyone valuable skills to last a lifetime. Bond over the bubbling pots and share stories while you wait for the timer to ding. With each 'pop' of the sealing jars, you'll feel like a kitchen superhero, and so will your friends! Let's spread the can-do spirit and start planning your first canning bash or crash-course in pickling. Who's ready to become a canning champion?

Canning Clubs and Community Events

So you've been through the first steps and jars of your canning journey, and I bet you're eager to dish out high-fives and share your crafty canned creations with the world. Well, guess what? There's a place for that, and it's not just your kitchen – welcome to the world of canning clubs and community events. It's like a superhero team-up but for preserving pros and jammers-in-training!

Imagine a place where mason jars are the stars and everyone speaks your language of lids and lifts. Starting a canning club or joining an existing one can rocket your skills from greenhorn to green-thumb faster than you can say 'pressure canner'! It's like having a circle of wise grandmas and keen kiddos, all ready to swap recipes and tips.

Why not kick things off by stitching together a spiffy canning club at your school or neighborhood? You don't need a fancy name, just a bunch of food adventurers eager to turn the earth's bounty into pantry treasures. Think of it as a book club, but instead of chapters, you're churning through chutneys and pickles!

Once you've gathered your gung-ho gang, it's time to plan your first event. Why not make it a 'Canning Carnival' or 'Preserve-a-Palooza'? Get creative with the name – it's all part of the fun! Line up some tables, pile up those fruits and veggies, and dive into a day of slicing, dicing, and delighting in the art of canning.

Community events like farmers' markets or neighborhood fairs are primo spots to show off your handiwork. Ever thought about setting up a booth? You can dish out samples of your jam-tastic strawberry jam or crunch-ilicious pickles, and maybe even demo the magic of sealing up summer in a jar.

Another stellar idea is to host a potluck where the main attraction is home-canned goods. It's a taste-testing extravaganza! Bring your best jar of apricot preserves and exchange it for a ribboned jar of somebody's secret-recipe salsa. You're not just swapping jars; you're trading secrets, stories, and smiles.

Don't forget to loop in the local legends – your town's veteran canners. Let them take the stage (or the front of your picnic table) to share their tried-and-true tricks. It's like passing down a torch of tradition through tales of triumphs and the occasional explosive tomato – metaphorically speaking, of course.

When the holidays roll around, community events kick up a notch. Themed canning parties? Yes, please! Whether it's "Spooky Preserves" for Halloween or "Festive Fruits" for the holiday season, tie on that apron with a seasonal twist. You'll be surprised how many peeps will jump on the jar wagon when there's a dash of holiday spirit involved.

Let's not forget about giving back. How about canning for a cause? Team up with a local shelter or food pantry and dedicate a day to canning soups, veggies, and fruits for those who need a bit more love and nutrition on their plates. It's heartwarming work that chimes with the very essence of community.

Oh, and who could forget the competitions? County fair, here you come! Whether you get ribbons or not, entering your canned goods in a local contest gets the community buzzin'. Plus, the judges' feedback is like gold dust to help spruce up your skills.

Now, if you're thinking big (and why not?), coordinate a 'Canning Camp' during summer or fall break. It could be a day or a week-long fiesta of fruits, tomatoes, jellies, and jams. Mix in some outdoor fun, and voila, you've got yourself a recipe for unforgettable foodie memories.

Remember, your canning club can leap beyond the local. The internet is a vast orchard ripe with fellow canning enthusiasts. Set up a blog or an online group to share your tales and pics of perfect preserves with chums from coast to coast!

Whether you're a lone ranger or a club captain, there's room for everyone in the world of canning clubs and community events. It's not just about the jars; it's about the journeys, the connections, and the sweet, tangy, and downright delicious things that happen when canners unite. So grab your gear, gather your crew, and get those community vibes flowing, because there's magic in sharing the craft of canning – one jar at a time.

Keep the Adventure Going!

Well, we've been through quite the journey, haven't we? Our cans are lined up like colorful little soldiers, guarding the fruits (and vegetables) of our labor. And while it may feel like the journey's ending, I'm here to tell you, the adventure is just getting started!

Remember when we learned that the history of canning is as rich as raspberry jam? It's cool to think that you're part of a tradition that goes back centuries, isn't it? Guess what? You're writing your own chapter in that history book now—just think of the stories you'll tell!

Each jar you sealed is brimming with more than just food—it's packed with the love you put into making it and the fun you had while doing so. You've turned simple ingredients into culinary gold and learned skills that will last a lifetime. That's something to puff your chest out about!

And, I've got to say, you've become quite the savvy safety expert! Sterilization isn't just a word you gloss over—it's your mantra. You know that canning without care is like trying to ride a bike with no wheels. But you, my friend, are fully equipped and pedaling forward.

Let's not forget the science of canning we delved into. What happens inside that jar is no less magical than a wizard's potion. You've observed science in action and harnessed it to create shelf-stable wonders—like a real kitchen scientist!

Starting with jams and jellies, you waded into the sweet waters of canning without fear. You mashed, you mixed, you created. Sweet, tangy, zesty—flavors danced on your tongue as you uncovered the joy of making something from scratch.

We then dived into the crunchy world of pickles and relishes, didn't we? You learned the delicate balance of sweet and sour and spiced up your life (and your sandwiches!) in the process. Customizing your own crunch was like tailoring your taste buds to a T.

Vegetables and soups found a home in jars under your watchful eye. No more will you wonder what's for dinner; a pantry full of homemade goodness awaits your decision. You've canned comfort and convenience, all in one.

Fruit canning? You conquered that like a champ. Peaches and pears took a dive into syrupy pools, emerging as jarred jewels. Every season can now be tasted year-round thanks to your fruity endeavors.

Tackling tomatoes, salsas, and sauces, you simmered, seasoned, and succeeded. You've turned the humble tomato into a masterpiece of flavor. Salsas and sauces? You're the artist; the kitchen's your canvas.

And, of course, we tapped into our creativity with unique ideas and recipes, making gifts that speak from the heart. Your canned goods are little ambassadors of your new-found skill, traveling to kitchens far and wide.

From your own garden to the jar, you understood the cycle of sustainable living. Planting, nurturing, harvesting, and preserving—it's a beautiful, rewarding circle that you're now a proud part of.

You've seen how community canning can turn what is often a solitary activity into a social bonanza. Sharing this journey with others just multiplies the fun and expands the learning—it's like turning up the volume on an already awesome song.

So as we close this chapter, I leave you with a full heart and a challenge: Keep seeking out new flavors, new techniques, and new adventures in canning. Experiment with different spices, try out unfamiliar produce, and maybe even grow an exotic fruit or vegetable for your next project.

Remember, every time you pop open a jar of your homemade goodness, you're not just savoring a delicious bite—you're feasting on memories and achievements. So keep that stove hot, those jars at the ready, and that spirit of adventure alive. The world of canning is vast and full of tastes undiscovered. Keep exploring, keep enjoying, and above all else, keep the adventure going!

Appendix A:
Measuring Guide and Conversions

Hey there, young chefs and canning enthusiasts! You've been on quite the journey – squishing fruits for jams, brining pickles, and blending salsas. But let's hit the pause button for a second and talk measuring and converting. Not the most exhilarating part of canning, but trust me, it's as essential as adding sugar to your strawberry jelly!

Measuring

When it comes to canning, precision is your best pal. Different ingredients need different measuring tools, so let's break it down:

Liquids: For water, vinegar, or that awesome syrup you're making, use liquid measuring cups. Fill it up, and check at eye level to make sure you're hitting the mark!

Dry ingredients: Flour, sugar, or spices? Scoop 'em with a dry measuring cup and level it off with the back of a knife for an exact amount.

Small stuff: Teaspoons and tablespoons are perfect for things like salt and herbs. Fill the spoon and sweep across the top to level it.

Conversions

Picture this: you're following a recipe that talks in ounces, but your scale has a mind of its own and only speaks in grams. Don't panic! Conversions to the rescue!

Liquid Volume: Remember, 1 cup equals 8 fluid ounces or about 237 milliliters. Whether you see a recipe in cups, ounces, or milliliters, just use this trick and you'll be golden.

Weight: If you've got 1 ounce, that's the same as 28.35 grams. Handy for when you have to weigh that pile of fruit for the perfect jelly ratio.

Temperature: Is the recipe feeling moody and using Celsius? Just multiply it by 1.8 (or double it and take away a tenth) and add 32. That's your Fahrenheit!

Now that you've got these tricks under your hat, you can measure and convert like a pro! Just think of it as one more secret ingredient in your canning cookbook. Equipped with a trusty measuring cup in one hand and this guide in the other, you're all set to tackle recipes from every corner of the globe.

Keep cooking, keep canning, and remember – every half-teaspoon and every milliliter counts towards making your canned creations the envy of the kitchen! Happy canning!

Appendix B:
Troubleshooting Your Canning

Okay, so you've been riding the canning rollercoaster: you've prepped, boiled, filled, and sealed. But wait a sec, something's not quite right when you take a peek at your canning creations. Don't worry, you're not alone! Sometimes things get a little wobbly in the canning world, but that's just part of the adventure. Let's go through some common canning hiccups and how to fix them, so you can get back to being a canning champ!

Lid Woes

Ever finished a batch and found a stubborn lid that just won't seal? Double-check that the rim was clean before setting the lid. If a seal failed after processing, don't worry, you've got options! Pop that jar in the fridge and enjoy it soon, or you can reprocess within 24 hours with a new, clean lid.

Cloudy or Floaty Bits

Finding your jars looking a tad cloudy or stuff floating around? It might just be some minerals from the water or bits from the produce. It's usually not harmful but can affect flavor. For a clearer jar next time, try using distilled water and make sure you're washing and prepping your produce correctly.

The Uninvited Crunch

When your pickles have more crunch than an autumn leaf on the sidewalk, it might be because the brine's too strong or the cucumbers were over mature. To avoid pickles that double as jaw exercises, follow the recipe's vinegar and water ratios like it's your favorite dance choreography – precise and with a bit of flair!

Unwanted Guests: Molds and Yeasts

Uh oh, did you find some fuzzy or slimy squatters in your jars? That's a sign that something's off. Make sure you're sticking to the sterilization steps, use the correct amount of acid like lemon juice or vinegar, and process your jars for the right length of time.

Fruit Drift

It can be a bummer when the fruit in your jams or preserves decide to hang out at the top of the jar. Keep fruit from floating to the top by ensuring there's even heat distribution during processing and maybe giving the jar a gentle turn halfway through cooling (just don't shake it like a maraca).

Siphoning or Liquid Loss

If it looks like your jars are leaking magic canning juice during processing, that's siphoning. Be sure you're not overfilling the jars; a proper headspace is like personal space – totally necessary. And when processing, let the jars cool down in the canner for a bit before moving them out into the world.

Tough-skinned Tomatoes

Tomatoes with skins tougher than your favorite superhero? Blanche them before jarring, and those skins will slip off smoother than a banana peel on a comedy show.

Remember, canning is a skill that gets tastier with practice! If you hit a snag, it's not the end of your canning career, it's just a twist in your canning tale. Keep going, keep learning, and who knows – you might come up with your own troubleshooting tips to pass down to the next generation of canning aficionados! Happy canning!

Appendix C:
Resources for Further Learning

Phew! You've bottled up a storm and now you're a canning champ with a pantry full of delicious, self-made treats! But let's not stop there. It's super important to keep growing—and I mean that both in the garden and in your canning wisdom. So where can you go next to dig even deeper into the world of canning and preserving? Well, I've put together a treasure trove of extra resources that'll keep your kitchen bubbling and your mind churning with new ideas.

Books to Devour (Metaphorically, of Course)

Canning for a New Generation - This book is jam-packed with out-of-the-jar ideas that break the mold!

The All New Ball Book of Canning and Preserving - It's like the canning Bible, telling you everything you need and want to know!

Preserving by the Pint - Perfect for when you're not trying to feed an army and just want a little batch of something tasty.

Cool Websites

For the tech-savvy canners with a hunger for scrolling and clicking:

Home Canning (National Center for Home Food Preservation): Not only does it have a super official name, but it's also brimming with safe, scientifically-backed information on how to keep your canning game strong and secure.

Pick Your Own: A nifty site where you can learn where to pick fresh produce in your area, plus some rad canning tips.

YouTube – The Visual Recipe Book

If reading isn't your jam (get it?), and you're more of a visual learner, then YouTube can be a goldmine. There are buckets of channels where canners like you show off their chops. Just make sure to search for "home canning tutorials" and you'll find an endless array of step-by-step guides.

Canning Classes

Ever thought about getting out of the house to learn? Local community centers, kitchen supply stores, and even some grocers offer hands-on canning workshops. It's a great way to make friends, and hey, you might even find yourself in a pickle class. Who wouldn't want that?

Remember, Keep it Safe

Remember the most important ingredient of all—safety! So while you're out exploring these resources, don't forget to stick to the safe practices you've learned. Your future self will high-five you for it!

And there you have it! Your very own map to the treasure of knowledge beyond what we've jarred up in these pages. Use it wisely, have a ton of fun, and keep spreading the can-do attitude. The adventure is just beginning, and the jar is your oyster... or, well, you know what I mean. Happy canning!

Chapter 13:
Acknowledgements

Well, we've been through quite the adventure together, haven't we? We've boiled, sealed, and saved some deliciousness in jars, all the while learning the ropes of a skill that's as timeless as it is tasty. But, like the cherry on top of your favorite jam, there comes a time to tip our hats and thank those who've made this journey possible. So here goes our round of hearty cheers and sincere thank-you's to an awesome bunch!

First off, let's give a round of applause to all the kitchen magicians from yesteryears who figured out canning could keep our bellies happy and full, come rain or shine or the time of the year. Their cleverness has given us the gift that keeps on giving&elete;the art of preserving our favorite eats. And to those brilliant minds that refined and shared canning wisdom&emdashfrom the scientific sharps to the humble home cooks&emdashyou rock our world!

Big shout out to the can't-beat-'em team of kitchen safety champs!

Kids, canning safety is a big deal, and we've had some real pros keeping us on the right track. They're like the kitchen knights ensuring every jar is a stronghold of yum without any 'uh oh' moments. So here's a salute to all those meticulous rule-followers who remind us that sterilization and safety are always in style!

And what about the tools that make all this canning craftiness possible? Let's give a nod to the inventors of all those nifty gadgets and gizmos. The lids, jars, funnels, and tongs&elete;without them, we'd be in a real pickle (and not the tasty kind we love). High-five to those creators that make sure our gear is both fun and functional!

A jar of applause for the science whizzes who've explained the 'whys' behind the 'hows'! Understanding the cleverness inside the jar, with all those busy microorganisms and the battle of the boil, is like having a superhero knowledge on our side. Because of them, we're canning pros, not just enthusiasts!

Remember the tasty times we had squishing fruit for jams and jellies? Let's not forget the fruit farmers and the buzzing bees that work together to give us the sweet stars of our spreads. Your fruitastic efforts are the foundation of our pantry's colorful collection!

Can we talk pickles and relishes for a sec? Those tangy treats wouldn't be the same without the tradition-bearers who passed down the secret to the perfect crunch. And to the vegetable growers that bring us the freshest of the fresh&elete;your labor is the zest in our jars!

A heap of gratitude goes to the soup-and-veggie enthusiasts. You've not only filled our jars with goodness, but also warmed our tummies and hearts with your souperb recipes and veggie victories.

Let's not forget those whole fruit canning gurus&elete;the ones who taught us the tricks to keep peaches and pears at their prime. Thanks to you, our syrups are sweet and our seasonings are spiced just right!

Ta-da to the tomatophiles and salsa samurais! Your secret sauces and tantalizing tomato tips are now legends on our bookshelves. Your garden-to-jar alchemy has turned us all into salsa dancers in the kitchen&emdash;well, sort of!

For the creative cans and unique ideas&emdash;a toast to the innovation in us all. From oils that ooze tradition to the jars that double as gifts, you've made sure our cupboards are as inventive as they are delicious.

A garden full of gratitude to the green-thumbed gurus who show us the magic of growing our canning ingredients. Thanks to you, we're seeing&emdash;and tasting&emdash;the cycle of sustainable living full circle.

And a communal high-five to the fellowship of canners everywhere. Canning isn't just a kitchen caper; it's a community celebration. Thank you to the class leaders, the club organizers, and every single person who shows that canning is caring&emdash;and sharing!

As for those who keep the lights on and the stoves heated with their hard work behind the scenes&elete;you've got our unwavering gratitude. From wisdom-whispering librarians to our patient taste testers (better known as family and friends)&emdash;we couldn't have done it without your support and those 'just one more bite' moments.

And lastly, to you, our Jar Warriors–young, old, and everyone in between. Your enthusiasm for transforming fruits and veggies into jars of joy has made all the difference. Keep that passion bubbling, and remember, every time you pop open a jar, you're savoring more than just food; you're relishing a world of fresh, sustainable, and spirited living.

So here's to everyone who's been a part of our canning chronicle. Your contributions are the ingredients that make this book so jam-packed with love and good eats. Keep spreading that canning cheer&emdash;may your pantry always be full, your jars sealed tight, and your meals a delight!

Chapter 14:
About the Author

As we cap off this jar-tastic journey, it's time to peel back the lid and see who's been stirring the pot of preservation knowledge. Yep, that's right – we're digging into the story of the avid canner behind all these savory chapters.

I'm just a person who finds the magic in the hiss of sealing jars, the vibrant colors of pickles, and the sweet satisfaction of homemade jam. It all started with a dusty book on canning I found nestled between gardening magazines and cookbooks in my grandparent's basement. You could say it was love at first sight—or should I say, at first bite!

Remember the tangy joy of those pickles and relishes we chatted about? Those page-turners had me hooked, and not before long, I was up to my elbows in brine and bliss. It wasn't just about the tang for me — it was the twang of tradition, the sizzle of sustainability, and the jingle of jars lining up like soldiers ready to keep food fresh and delicious.

Last weekend's soup vanished into jars faster than a bunny at a lettuce convention. That story doesn't just tell you I've got a soup obsession (I mean, who doesn't?), but that canning has become second nature to me — just like it can for you. I'm here to show you that canning is the superhero of the kitchen, swooping in to save the day, meal preps, and your taste buds.

This love for canning spiced up my passion for teaching. Watching a newbie's eyes light up when they hear their first jar "ping!" is the kind of energy I live for. As an educator, bringing families and communities together over steaming pots and gardening plots became my strawberry jam – metaphorically and literally.

The practical benefits of canning, like slashing that grocery bill and nixing the preservatives, are just the cherry on top. When children learn to can, they don't just skill up — they wise up to the value of food, the effort it takes to grow it, and the joy of sharing it.

It's about living sustainably without skimping on the savory stuff. From my little urban garden plot, which is a testament to what you can do with just a sprinkle of space, to the countertops covered in every color the veggie spectrum can offer, this is the living portrait of sustainable eats.

Now, let me tell you a secret: You remember Chapter 10, where we jazzed up jars with unique ideas? That's the spirit I embody every day. While I'm not penning down my latest canning conquests or conjuring up culinary storms in my kitchen, I'm dreaming up new, zany flavors to jar next. Cilantro-lime peaches? Don't knock it 'till you try it!

This book is my love letter to canning and to all of you who've kept turning pages, eager for the next recipe or tip. Think of it as a jar filled with the finest ingredients — knowledge, fun, and the infectious energy of creation, all sealed with a pop!

My role extends beyond the kitchen. As a dedicated advocate for local farmers' markets and community gardens, I've seen firsthand how every small seed can bloom into a movement. You'll often catch me chattering away at local events or leading a gaggle of enthusiastic canners at a workshop, living my truth — that community and canning go together like peas and carrots.

One thing's certain: I'm just as much a learner as a teacher. Staying rooted in the community keeps me listening, growing, and innovating. Every question from a bright-eyed child or adult learner adds to my knowledge and fuels the fire for my next canventure.

Families who dive into this book, and the delicious world it brings to life, are families who find joy in the little things, like the crunch of a perfectly pickled bean or the burst of flavor from a spoonful of fresh jam. And to be able to contribute to that, to be a part of your family's journey into a more sustainable life — well, that's the juicy center of it all.

As we seal this chapter and you venture back into your kitchen, remember that the journey is just like canning itself – filled with trials, errors, and a bundle of pings of success. Keep those pots bubbling, and never forget: the world of canning is vast, vibrant, and always ready for one more batch of curious canners like you!

To our new canning enthusiasts, seasoned jar packers, and everyone sailing in this deliciously delightful preserve boat — remember, the adventure never truly ends. It just gets sealed up, ready to be reopened with every batch you create and every memory you preserve.

So, as you gather your jars and ready your ingredients, think of me not just as the author, but as your comrade in canning, your buddy in brine, your pal in preservation. Here's to the delicious memories we'll craft and the timeless traditions we'll continue, all from the humble workings of our own kitchens. Happy canning!

Made in the USA
Monee, IL
29 August 2024

64864361R00049